The Lonely Dancer and Other Poems by Richard Le Gallienne

Richard Thomas Gallienne was born in Liverpool on 20th January, 1866.

His first job was in an accountant's office, but this was quickly abandoned to pursue his first love as a professional writer. His first work, My Ladies' Sonnets, was published in 1887.

In 1889 he became, for a brief time, literary secretary to Wilson Barrett the manager, actor, and playwright. Barrett enjoyed immense success with the staging of melodramas, which would later reach a peak with the historical tragedy The Sign of the Cross (1895).

Le Gallienne joined the staff of The Star newspaper in 1891, and also wrote for various other papers under the pseudonym 'Logroller'. He contributed to the short-lived but influential quarterly periodical The Yellow Book, published between 1894 and 1897.

His first wife, Mildred Lee, died in 1894 leaving their daughter, Hesper, in his care.

In 1897 he married the Danish journalist Julie Norregard. However, the marriage would not be a success. She left him in 1903 and took their daughter Eva to live in Paris. They were eventually divorced in June 1911.

Le Gallienne now moved to the United States and became resident there.

On 27th October 1911, he married Mrs. Irma Perry, whose marriage to her first cousin, the painter and sculptor Roland Hinton Perry, had been dissolved in 1904. Le Gallienne and Irma had known each other for many years and had written an article together a few years earlier in 1906.

Le Gallienne and Irma lived in Paris from the late 1920s, where Irma's daughter Gwen was by then an established figure in the expatriate bohème. Le Gallienne also added a regular newspaper column to the frequent publication of his poems, essays and other articles.

By 1930 Le Gallienne's book publishing career had virtually ceased. During the latter years of that decade Le Gallienne lived in Menton on the French Riviera and, during the war years, in nearby Monaco. His house was commandeered by German troops and his handsome library was nearly sent back to Germany as bounty. Le Gallienne managed a successful appeal to a German officer in Monaco which allowed him to return to Menton to collect his books.

To his credit Le Gallienne refused to write propaganda for the local German and Italian authorities, and financially was often in dire need. On one occasion he collapsed in the street due to hunger.

Richard Thomas Gallienne died on 15th September 1947. He is buried in Menton in a grave whose lease is, at present, due to expire in 2023.

Not all my treasure hath the bandit Time
Locked in his glimmering caverns of the Past:
Fair women dead and friendships of old rhyme,
And noble dreams that had to end at last:—

Ah! these indeed; and from youth's sacristy
Full many a holy relic hath he torn,
Vessels of mystic faith God filled for me,
Holding them up to Him in life's young morn.

All these are mine no more—Time hath them all,
Time and his adamantine gaoler Death:
Despoilure vast—yet seemeth it but small,
When unto thee I turn, thy bloom and breath
Filling with light and incense the last shrine,
Innermost, inaccessible,—yea, thine.

Index of Contents

THE LONELY DANCER

I had no heart to join the dance,
I danced it all so long ago—
Ah! light-winged music out of France,
Let other feet glide to and fro,
Weaving new patterns of romance
For bosoms of new-fallen snow.

But leave me thus where I may hear
The leafy rustle of the waltz,
The shell-like murmur in my ear,
The silken whisper fairy-false
Of unseen rainbows circling near,
And the glad shuddering of the walls.

Another dance the dancers spin,
A shadow-dance of mystic pain,
And other partners enter in
And dance within my lonely brain—
The swaying woodland shod in green,
The ghostly dancers of the rain;

The lonely dancers of the sea,
Foam-footed on the sandy bar,
The wizard dance of wind and tree,
The eddying dance of stream and star;
Yea, all these dancers tread for me
A measure mournful and bizarre:

An echo-dance where ear is eye,
And sound evokes the shapes of things,
Where out of silence and a sigh
The sad world like a picture springs,
As, when some secret bird sweeps by,
We see it in the sound of wings.

Those human feet upon the floor,
That eager pulse of rhythmic breath,—
How sadly to an unknown shore
Each silver footfall hurryeth;
A dance of autumn leaves, no more,
On the fantastic wind of death.

Fire clasped to elemental fire,
'Tis thus the solar atom whirls;
The butterfly in aery gyre,
On autumn mornings, swarms and swirls,
In dance of delicate desire,
No other than these boys and girls.

The same strange music everywhere,
The woven paces just the same,
Dancing from out the viewless air
Into the void from whence they came;
Ah! but they make a gallant flare
Against the dark, each little flame!

And what if all the meaning lies
Just in the music, not in those
Who dance thus with transfigured eyes,
Holding in vain each other close;
Only the music never dies,
The dance goes on,—the dancer goes.

A woman dancing, or a world
Poised on one crystal foot afar,
In shining gulfs of silence whirled,
Like notes of the strange music are;
Small shape against another curled,
Or dancing dust that makes a star.

To him who plays the violin
All one it is who joins the reel,
Drops from the dance, or enters in;
So that the never-ending wheel
Cease not its mystic course to spin,
For weal or woe, for woe or weal.

I

FLOS AEVORUM

You must mean more than just this hour,
You perfect thing so subtly fair,
Simple and complex as a flower,
Wrought with such planetary care;
How patient the eternal power
That wove the marvel of your hair.

How long the sunlight and the sea
Wove and re-wove this rippling gold
To rhythms of eternity;
And many a flashing thing grew old,
Waiting this miracle to be;
And painted marvels manifold,

Still with his work unsatisfied,
Eager each new effect to try,
The solemn artist cast aside,
Rainbow and shell and butterfly,
As some stern blacksmith scatters wide
The sparks that from his anvil fly.

How many shells, whorl within whorl,
Litter the marges of the sphere
With wrack of unregarded pearl,
To shape that little thing your ear:
Creation, just to make one girl,
Hath travailed with exceeding fear.

The moonlight of forgotten seas
Dwells in your eyes, and on your tongue
The honey of a million bees,
And all the sorrows of all song:
You are the ending of all these,
The world grew old to make you young.

All time hath traveled to this rose;
To the strange making of this face
Came agonies of fires and snows;
And Death and April, nights and days
Unnumbered, unimagined throes,
Find in this flower their meeting place.

Strange artist, to my aching thought
Give answer: all the patient power
That to this perfect ending wrought,
Shall it mean nothing but an hour?
Say not that it is all for nought
Time brings Eternity a flower.

All the words in all the world
Cannot tell you how I love you,
All the little stars that shine
To make a silver crown above you;

"ALL THE WORDS IN ALL THE WORLD"

All the flowers cannot weave
A garland worthy of your hair,
Not a bird in the four winds
Can sing of you that is so fair.

Only the spheres can sing of you;
Some planet in celestial space,
Hallowed and lonely in the dawn,
Shall sing the poem of your face.

"I SAID—I CARE NOT"

I said—I care not if I can
But look into her eyes again,
But lay my hand within her hand
Just once again.

Though all the world be filled with snow
And fire and cataclysmal storm,
I'll cross it just to lay my head
Upon her bosom warm.

Ah! bosom made of April flowers,
Might I but bring this aching brain,
This foolish head, and lay it down
On April once again!

"ALL THE WIDE WORLD IS BUT THE THOUGHT OF YOU"

All the wide world is but the thought of you:
Who made you out of wonder and of dew?
Was it some god with tears in his deep eyes,
Who loved a woman white and over-wise,
That strangely put all violets in your hair—
And put into your face all distance too?

"LIGHTNINGS MAY FLICKER ROUND MY HEAD"

Lightnings may flicker round my head,
And all the world seem doom,
If you, like a wild rose, will walk
Strangely into the room.

If only my sad heart may hear
Your voice of faery laughter—
What matters though the heavens fall,

And hell come thundering after.

"THE AFTERNOON IS LONELY FOR YOUR FACE"

The afternoon is lonely for your face,
The pampered morning mocks the day's decline—
I was so rich at noon, the sun was mine,
Mine the sad sea that in that rocky place
Girded us round with blue betrothal ring.
Because your heart was mine, your heart, that precious thing.

The night will be a desert till the dawn,
Unless you take some ferry-boat of dreams,
And glide to me, a glory of silver beams,
Under my eyelids, like sad curtains drawn;
So, by good hap, my heart can find its way
Where all your sweetness lies in fragrant disarray.

Ah! but with morn the world begins anew,
Again the sea shall sing up to your feet,
And earth and all the heavens call you sweet,
You all alone with me, I all alone with you,
And all the business of the laurelled hours
Shyly to gaze on that betrothal ring of ours.

"SORE IN NEED WAS I OF A FAITHFUL FRIEND"

Sore in need was I of a faithful friend,
And it seemed to me that life
Had come to its much desired end—
Just then God gave me a wife.

I had seen the beauty of fairy things,
And seen the women walk;
I had heard the voice of the seven sins
And all the wonderful talk.

Ah, the promising earth that seems so kind,
And the comrades with outstretched hand—
But did you ever stand alone
In a black, forsaken land?
Then the wonderful things that God can do
One comes to understand:

How He turns the desert dust to a dream,
And the lonely wind to a friend,
And makes a bright beginning
Of what had seemed the end:
'Twas in such an hour God placed in mine
The moonbeam hand of a friend.

"I THOUGHT, BEFORE MY SUNLIT TWENTIETH YEAR"

I thought, before my sunlit twentieth year,
That I knew Love, and Death that goes with it;
And my young broken heart in little songs,
Dew-like, I poured, and waited for my end
Wildly—and waited—being then nineteen.
I walked a little longer on my way,
Alive, 'gainst expectation and desire,
And, being then past twenty, I beheld
The face of all the faces of the world
Dewily opening on its stem for me.
Ah! so it seemed, and, each succeeding year,
Thus hath some woman blossom of the divine
Flowered in my path, and made a frail delay
In my true journey—to my home in thee.

October 27, 1911.

II

TO A BIRD AT DAWN

O bird that somewhere yonder sings,
In the dim hour 'twixt dreams and dawn,
Lone in the hush of sleeping things,
In some sky sanctuary withdrawn;
Your perfect song is too like pain,
And will not let me sleep again.

I think you must be more than bird,
A little creature of soft wings,
Not yours this deep and thrilling word—
Some morning planet 'tis that sings;
Surely from no small feathered throat
Wells that august, eternal note.

As some old language of the dead,
In one resounding syllable,
Says Rome and Greece and all is said—
A simple word a child may spell;
So in your liquid note impearled
Sings the long epic of the world.

Unfathomed sweetness of your song,
With ancient anguish at its core,
What womb of elemental wrong,
With shudder unimagined, bore
Peace so divine—what hell hath trod
This voice that softly talks with God!

All silence in one silver flower
Of speech that speaks not, save as speaks
The moon in heaven, yet hath power
To tell the soul the thing it seeks.
And pack, as by some wizard's art,
The whole within the finite part.

To you, sweet bird, one well might feign—
With such authority you sing
So clear, yet so profound, a strain
Into the simple ear of spring—
Some secret understanding given
Of the hid purposes of Heaven.

And all my life until this day,
And all my life until I die,
All joy and sorrow of the way,
Seem calling yonder in the sky;
And there is something the song saith
That makes me unafraid of death.

Now the slow light fills all the trees,
The world, before so still and strange,
With day's familiar presences,
Back to its common self must change,
And little gossip shapes of song
The porches of the morning throng.

Not yours with such as these to vie
That of the day's small business sing,
Voice of man's heart and of God's sky—
But O you make so deep a thing
Of joy, I dare not think of pain
Until I hear you sing again.

ALMA VENUS

Only a breath—hardly a breath! The shore
Is still a huddled alabaster floor
Of shelving ice and shattered slabs of cold,
Stern wreckage of the fiercely frozen wave,
Gleaming in mailed wastes of white and gold;
As though the sea, in an enchanted grave,
Of fearful crystal locked, no more shall stir
Softly, all lover, to the April moon:
Hardly a breath! yet was I now aware
Of a most delicate balm upon the air,
Almost a voice that almost whispered "soon"!

Not of the earth it was—no living thing
Moves in the iron landscape far or near,
Saving, in raucous flight, the winter crow,
Staining the whiteness with its ebon wing,
Or silver-sailing gull, or 'mid the drear
Rock cedars, like a summer soul astray,
A lone red squirrel makes believe to play,
Nibbling the frozen snow.

Not of the earth, that hath not scent nor song,
Nor hope of aught, nor memory, nor dream,
Nor any speech upon its sullen tongue,
Nor any liberty of running stream;
Not of the earth, that hath forgot to smile;
But, strangely wafted o'er the frozen sea,
As from some hidden Cytherean isle,
Veil within veil, the sweetness came to me.

Beyond the heaving glitter of the floe,
The free blue water sparkles to the sky,
Losing itself in brightness; to and fro
Long bands of mists trail luminously by,
And, as behind a screen, on the sea's rim
Hid softnesses of sunshine come and go,
And shadowy coasts in sudden glory swim—
O land made out of distance and desire!—
With ports of mystic pearl and crests of fire.

Thence, somewhere in the spaces of the sea,
Travelled this halcyon breath presaging Spring;
Over the water even now secretly

She maketh ready in her hands to bring
Blossom and blade and wing;
And soon the wave shall ripple with her feet,
And her wild hair be blown about the skies,

And with her bosom all the world grow sweet,
And blue with the sea-blue of her deep eyes
The meadow, like another sea, shall flower,
And all the earth be song and singing shower;
While watching, in some hollow of the grass
By the sea's edge, I may behold her stand,
With rosy feet, upon the yellow sand,
Pause in a dream, and to the woodland pass.

"AH! DID YOU EVER HEAR THE SPRING"

Ah! did you ever hear the Spring
Calling you through the snow,
Or hear the little blackbird sing
Inside its egg—or go
To that green land where grass begins,
Each tiny seed, to grow?

O have you heard what none has heard,
Or seen what none has seen;
O have you been to that strange land
Where no one else has been!

APRIL

April, half-clad in flowers and showers,
Walks, like a blossom, o'er the land;
She smiles at May, and laughing takes
The rain and sunshine hand in hand.

So gay the dancing of her feet,
So like a garden her soft breath,
So sweet the smile upon her face,
She charms the very heart of death.

The young moon in a trance she holds
Captive in clouds of orchard bloom,
She snaps her fingers at the grave,
And laughs into the face of doom.

Yet in her gladness lurks a fear,
In all her mirth there breathes a sigh,
So soon her pretty flowers are gone—
And ah! she is too young to die!

MAY IS BUILDING HER HOUSE

May is building her house. With apple blooms
She is roofing over the glimmering rooms;
Of the oak and the beech hath she builded its beams,
And, spinning all day at her secret looms,
With arras of leaves each wind-swayed wall
She pictureth over, and peopleth it all
With echoes and dreams,
And singing of streams.

May is building her house of petal and blade;
Of the roots of the oak is the flooring made,
With a carpet of mosses and lichen and clover,
Each small miracle over and over,
And tender, travelling green things strayed.

Her windows the morning and evening star,
And her rustling doorways, ever ajar
With the coming and going
Of fair things blowing,
The thresholds of the four winds are.

May is building her house. From the dust of things
She is making the songs and the flowers and the wings;
From October's tossed and trodden gold
She is making the young year out of the old;
Yea! out of winter's flying sleet
She is making all the summer sweet,
And the brown leaves spurned of November's feet
She is changing back again to spring's.

SHADOW

When leaf and flower are newly made,
And bird and butterfly and bee
Are at their summer posts again;
When all is ready, lo! 'tis she,

Suddenly there after soft rain—
The deep-lashed dryad of the shade.

Shadow! the fairest gift of June,
Gone like the rose the winter through,
Save in the ribbed anatomy
Of ebon line the moonlight drew,
Stark on the snow, of tower or tree,
Like letters of a dead man's rune.

Dew-breathing shade! all summer lies
In the cool hollow of thy breast,
Thou moth-winged creature darkly fair;
The very sun steals down to rest
Within thy swaying tendrilled hair,
And forest-flicker of thine eyes.

Made of all shapes that flit and sway,
And mass, and scatter in the breeze,
And meet and part, open and close;
Thou sister of the clouds and trees,
Thou daintier phantom of the rose,
Thou nun of the hot and honeyed day.

Misdeemed art thou of those who hold
Darkness thy soul, thy dwelling place
Night and its stars; nay! all of light
Wert though begot, all flowers thy face,
And, hushed in thee, all colours bright
Hide from the noon their blue and gold.

Thy voice the song of hidden rills,
The sigh deep-bosomed silence heaves
From the full heart of happy things,—
The lap of water-lily leaves,
The noiseless language of the wings
Of evening making strange the hills.

JUNE

We thought that winter, love, would never end,
That the dark year had slain the innocent May,
Nor hoped that your soft hand, this summer day,
Would lie, as now, in mine, beloved friend;
And, like some magic spring, your dream-deep eyes
Hold all the summer skies.

But lo! the world again is mad with flowers,
The long white silence spake, small bird by bird,
Blade after blade, amid the song of showers,
The grass stole back once more, and there was heard
The ancient music of the vernal spheres,
Half laughter and half tears.

Ah! love, and now too swiftly, like some groom,
Raining hot kisses on his bride's young mouth,
The mad young year, delirious with the South,
Squanders his fairy treasure, bloom on bloom;
Too soon the wild rose hastens to be sweet,
Too swift, O June, thy feet.

Tarry a little, summer, crowd not so
All glory and gladness in so brief a day,
Teach all thy dancing flowers a step more slow,
And bid thy wild musicians softlier play,
O hast thou thought, that like a madman spends,
The longest summer ends.

GREEN SILENCE

Silence, whose drowsy eyelids are soft leaves,
And whose half-sleeping eyes are the blue flowers,
On whose still breast the water-lily heaves,
For all her speech the whisper of the showers.

Made of all things that in the water sway,
The quiet reed kissing the arrowhead,
The willows murmuring, all a summer day,
"Silence"—sweet word, and ne'er so softly said

As here along this path of brooding peace,
Where all things dream, and nothing else is done
But all such gentle businesses as these
Of leaves and rippling wind, and setting sun

Turning the stream to a long lane of gold,
Where the young moon shall walk with feet of pearl,
And, framed in sleeping lilies, fold on fold,
Gaze at herself, like any mortal girl.

SUMMER SONGS

I

How thick the grass,
How green the shade—
All for love
And lovers made.

Wood-lilies white
As hidden lace—
Open your bodice,
That's their place.

See how the sun-god
Overpowers
The summer lying
Deep in flowers;

With burning kisses
Of bright gold
Fills her young womb
With joy untold;

And all the world
Is lad and lass,
A blue sky
And a couch of grass.

Summer is here—
let us drain
It all! it may
Not come again.

II

How the leaves thicken
On the boughs,
And the birds make
Their lyric vows.

O the beating, breaking
Heart of things,
The pulse and passion—
How it sings.

How it burns and flames

And showers,
Lusts and laughs, flowers
And deflowers.

III

Summer came,
Rose on rose;
Leaf on leaf,
Summer goes.

Summer came,
Song on song;
O summer had
A golden tongue.

Summer goes,
Sigh on sigh;
Not a rose
Sees him die.

TO A WILD BIRD

Wild bird, I stole you from your nest,
And cannot find your nest again;
To hear you chirp a little while
I wrung your mother's heart with pain.

And here you sit and droop and die,
Nor any love that I can bring
Wins me forgiveness for the wrong,
Nor any kindness makes you sing.

"I CROSSED THE ORCHARD WALKING HOME"

I crossed the orchard, walking home,
The rising moon was at my back,
The apples and the moonlight fell
Together on the railroad track.

Then, speeding through the evening dews,
A dozen lighted windows glide—
The East-bound flyer for New York,

Soft as a magic-lantern slide.

New York! on through the sleeping flowers,
Through echoing midnight on to noon;
How strange that yonder is New York,
And here such silence and the moon.

"I MEANT TO DO MY WORK TO-DAY"

I meant to do my work to-day—
But a brown bird sang in the apple-tree,
And a butterfly flitted across the field,
And all the leaves were calling me.

And the wind went sighing over the land,
Tossing the grasses to and fro,
And a rainbow held out its shining hand—
So what could I do but laugh and go?

"HOW FAST THE YEAR IS GOING BY"

How fast the year is going by!
Love, it will be September soon;
O let us make the best of June.
Already, love, it is July;
The rose and honeysuckle go,
And all too soon will come the snow.

Dark berries take the place of flowers,
Of summer August still remains,
Then sad September with her rains.
O love, how short a year is ours—
So swiftly does the summer fly,
Scarce time is left to say goodbye.

AUGUST MOONLIGHT

The solemn light behind the barns,
The rising moon, the cricket's call,
The August night, and you and I—
What is the meaning of it all!

Has it a meaning, after all?
Or is it one of Nature's lies,
That net of beauty that she casts
Over Life's unsuspecting eyes?

That web of beauty that she weaves
For one strange purpose of her own,—
For this the painted butterfly,
For this the rose—for this alone!

Strange repetition of the rose,
And strange reiterated call
Of bird and insect, man and maid,—
Is that the meaning of it all?

If it means nothing, after all!
And nothing lives, except to die—
It is enough—that solemn light
Behind the barns, and you and I.

TO A ROSE

O rose! forbear to flaunt yourself,
All bloom and dew—
I once, sad-hearted as I am,
Was young as you.

But, one by one, the petals fell
Earthward to rot;
Only a berry testifies
A rose forgot.

INVITATION

Unless you come while still the world is green,
A place of birds and the blue dreaming sea,
In vain has all the singing summer been,
Unless you come, and share it all with me.

Ah! come, ere August flames its heart away,
Ere, like a golden widow, autumn goes
Across the woodlands, sad with thoughts of May,
An aster in her bosom for a rose.

SUMMER GOING

Crickets calling,
Apples falling.

Summer dying,
Life is flying.

So soon over—
Love and lover.

AUTUMN TREASURE

Who will gather with me the fallen year,
This drift of forgotten forsaken leaves,
Ah! who give ear
To the sigh October heaves
At summer's passing by!
Who will come walk with me
On this Persian carpet of purple and gold
The weary autumn weaves,
And be as sad as I?
Gather the wealth of the fallen rose,
And watch how the memoried south wind blows
Old dreams and old faces upon the air,
And all things fair.

WINTER

Winter, some call thee fair,
Yea! flatter thy cold face
With vain compare
Of all thy glittering ways
And magic snows
With summer and the rose;
Thy phantom flowers
And fretted traceries
Of crystal breath,
Thy frozen and fantastic art of death,
With April as she showers
The violet on the leas,
And bares her bosom

In the blossoming trees,
And dances on her way
To laugh with May—
Winter that hath no bird
To sing thee, and no bloom
To deck thy brow:
To me thou art an empty haunted room,
Where once the music
Of the summer stirred,
And all the dancers
Fallen on silence now.

THE MYSTIC FRIENDS

I nothing did all yesterday
But listen to the singing rain
On roof and weeping window-pane,
And, 'whiles I'd watch the flying spray
And smoking breakers in the bay:
Nothing but this did I all day—

Save turn anon to trim the fire
With a new log, and mark it roar
And flame with yellow tongues for more
To feed its mystical desire.
No other comrades save these three,
The fire, the rain, and the wild sea,

All day from morn till night had I—
Yea! and the wind, with fitful cry,
Like a hound whining at the door.

Yet seemed it, as to sleep I turned,
Pausing a little while to pray,
That not mis-spent had been the day;
That I had somehow wisdom learned
From those wild waters in the bay,
And from the fire as it burned;
And that the rain, in some strange way,
Had words of high import to say;
And that the wind, with fitful cry,
Did some immortal message try,
Striving to make some meaning clear
Important for my soul to hear.

But what the meaning of the rain,

And what the wisdom of the fire,
And what the warning of the wind,
And what the sea would tell, in vain
My soul doth of itself enquire,—
And yet a meaning too doth find:

For what am I that hears and sees
But a strange brother of all these
That blindly move, and wordless cry,
And I, mysteriously I,
Answer in blood and bone and breath
To what my gnomic kindred saith;
And, as in me they all have part,
Translate their message to my heart—

And know, yet know not, what they say:
Know not, yet know, the fire's tongue
And the rain's elegiac song,
And the white language of the spray,
And all the wind meant yesterday—
Yea! wiser he, when the day ends,
Who shared it with those four strange friends.

THE COUNTRY GODS

I dwell, with all things great and fair:
The green earth and the lustral air,
The sacred spaces of the sea,
Day in, day out, companion me.
Pure-faced, pure-thoughted, folk are mine
With whom to sit and laugh and dine;
In every sunlit room is heard
Love singing, like an April bird,
And everywhere the moonlit eyes
Of beauty guard our paradise;
While, at the ending of the day,
To the kind country gods we pray,
And dues of our fair living pay.

Thus, when, reluctant, to the town
I go, with country sunshine brown,
So small and strange all seems to me—
the boonfellow of the sea—
That these town-people say and be:
Their insect lives, their insect talk,
Their busy little insect walk,

Their busy little insect stings—
And all the while the sea-weed swings
Against the rock, and the wide roar
Rises foam-lipped along the shore.
Ah! then how good my life I know,
How good it is each day to go
Where the great voices call, and where
The eternal rhythms flow and flow.
In that august companionship,
The subtle poisoned words that drip,
With guileless guile, from friendly lip,
The lie that flits from ear to ear,
Ye shall not speak, ye shall not hear;
Nor shall you fear your heart to say,
Lest he who listens shall betray.

The man who hearkens all day long
To the sea's cosmic-thoughted song
Comes with purged ears to lesser speech,
And something of the skyey reach
Greatens the gaze that feeds on space;
The starlight writes upon his face
That bathes in starlight, and the morn
Chrisms with dew, when day is born,
The eyes that drink the holy light
Welling from the deep springs of night.

And so—how good to catch the train
Back to the country gods again.

III

TO ONE ON A JOURNEY

Why did you go away without one word,
Wave of the hand, or token of good-bye,
Nor leave some message for me with flower or bird,
Some sign to find you by;

Some stray of blossom on the winter road,
To know your feet had gone that very way,
Told me the star that points to your abode,
And tossed me one faint ray

To climb from out the night where now I
dwell—

Or, seemed it best for you to go alone
To heaven, as alone I go to hell
Upon the four winds blown.

HER PORTRAIT IMMORTAL

Must I believe this beauty wholly gone
That in her picture here so deathless seems,
And must I henceforth speak of her as one
Tells of some face of legend or of dreams,
Still here and there remembered—scarce believed,
Or held the fancy of a heart bereaved.

So beautiful she—was; ah! "was," say I,
Yet doubt her dead—I did not see her die.
Only by others borne across the sea
Came the incredible wild blasphemy
They called her death—as though it could be true
Of such an immortality as you!

True of these eyes that from her picture gaze,
Serene, star-steadfast, as the heaven's own eyes;
Of that deep bosom, white as hawthorn sprays,
Where my world-weary head forever lies;
True of these quiet hands, so marble-cool,
Still on her lap as lilies on a pool.

Must I believe her dead—that this sweet clay,
That even from her picture breathes perfume,
Was carried on a fiery wind away,
Or foully locked in the worm-whispering tomb;
This casket rifled, ribald fingers thrust
'Mid all her dainty treasure—is this dust!

Once such a dewy marvel of a girl,
Warm as the sun, and ivory as the moon;
All gone of her, all lost—except this curl
Saved from her head one summer afternoon,
Tied with a little ribbon from her breast—
This only mine, and Death's now all the rest.

Must I believe it true! Bid me not go
Where on her grave the English violets blow;
Nay, leave me—if a dream, indeed, it be—
Still in my dream that she is somewhere she,
Silent, as was her wont. It is a lie—

She is not dead—I did not see her die.

SPRING'S PROMISES

When the spring comes again, will you be there?
Three springs I watched and waited for your face,
And listened for your voice upon the air;
I sought for you in many a hidden place,
Saying, "She must be there."

"Surely some magic slumber holds her fast,
She whose blue eyes were morning's earliest flowers,"
I sighed: and, one by one, before me passed
The rainbowed daughters of the vernal showers,
Saying, "She comes at last."

Ah! broken promise of the world! how fair
You speak young hearts! In many a wanton word
Of lyric April, each succeeding year,
By risen flower, and the returning bird,
You vowed to bring back her.

And now the flutes are in the trees once more,
The violets breathe up through the melting snow,
Old Earth throws open wide her grassy door—
As if there were no violets long ago,
Or any birds before.

"APRIL IS IN THE WORLD AGAIN"

April is in the world again,
And all the world is filled with flowers—
Flowers for others, not for me!
For my one flower I cannot see,
Lost in the April showers.

I cannot wake her, though I sing,
And all the birds, for her dear sake,
Fill with their songs the wintry brake;
Ah! could they make her rise again,
What resurrection would be mine!
Is she too tired to help the sun
And all the little stars to shine?

"SINGING GO I"

Singing go I, seeking for ever a song
Sung long ago; I ask no more to hear
Her voice that sang—for I should do her wrong,
Had I the power, to bring her once more near—

Near to the earth, its sorrow or its joy,
To drag her back into the arms of pain
And Love and all the April flowers again
And all her little dreams of heaven destroy.

Have I the heart? Ah! had I but the song,
The nightingale would listen and all things
That talk in waterfalls and trees and strings
Would hush themselves to listen as I sang,
Had I the song.

"WHO WAS IT SWEPT AGAINST MY DOOR"

Who was it swept against my door just now,
With rustling robes like Autumn's—was it thou?
Ah! would it were thy gown against my door—
Only thy gown once more.

Sometimes the snow, sometimes the fluttering breath
Of April, as toward May she wandereth,
Make me a moment think that it is thou—
But yet it is not thou!

"FACE IN THE TOMB THAT LIES SO STILL"

Face in the tomb, that lies so still,
May I draw near,
And watch your sleep and love you,
Without word or tear.

You smile, your eyelids flicker;
Shall I tell
How the world goes that lost you?
Shall I tell?

Ah! love, lift not your eyelids;
'Tis the same
Old story that we laughed at,—
Still the same.

We knew it, you and I,
We knew it all:
Still is the small the great,
The great the small;

Still the cold lie quenches
The flaming truth,
And still embattled age
Wars against youth.

Yet I believe still in the ever-living God
That fills your grave with perfume,
Writing your name in violets across the sod,
Shielding your holy face from hail and snow;
And, though the withered stay, the lovely go,
No transitory wrong or wrath of things
Shatters the faith—that each slow minute brings

That meadow nearer to us where your feet
Shall flicker near me like white butterflies—
That meadow where immortal lovers meet,
Gazing for ever in immortal eyes.

"I KNOW NOT IN WHAT PLACE"

I know not in what place again I'll meet
The face I love—but there is not a street
In the wide world where you can wander, sweet,
Without my finding you, with those great eyes;
Nor is there any star in all the skies
Can give you shelter from my pitiless love.

RESURRECTION

Is it your face I see, your voice I hear?
Your face, your voice, again after these years!
O is your cheek once more against my cheek?
And is this blessed rain, angel, your tears?

You have come back,—how strange—out of the grave;
Its dreams are in your eyes, and still there clings
Dust of the grave on your vainglorious hair;
And a mysterious rust is on these rings—

The ring we gave each other, that young night
When the moon rose on our betrothal kiss;
When the sun rose upon our wedding day,
How wonderful it was to give you this!

I dreamed you were a bird or a wild flower,
Some changed lovely thing that was not you;
Maybe, I said, she is the morning star,
A radiance unfathomably far—

And now again you are so strangely near!
Your face, your voice, again after these years!
Is it your face I see, your voice I hear,
And is this blessed rain, angel, your tears?

"WHEN THE LONG DAY HAS FADED"

When the long day has faded to its end,
The flowers gone, and all the singing done,
And there is no companion left save Death—
Ah! there is one,
Though in her grave she lies this many a year,
Will send a violet made of her blue eyes,
A flowering whisper of her April breath,
Up through the sleeping grass to comfort me,
And in the April rain her tears shall fall.

"HER EYES ARE BLUEBELLS NOW"

Her eyes are bluebells now, her voice a bird,
And the long sighing grass her elegy;
She who a woman was is now a star
In the high heaven shining down on me.

"THE DEAD AROSE"

The dead arose. Long had they dreamed,

Deep in the grass of the still grave,
Of meeting their beloved once more.
They knocked at each familiar door.
They waited eagerly to see
The old loved faces at the door,
They waited for a voice to say
The same old words it said before—
They knocked at each familiar door.
But no one answered to the dead,
No voice of welcome, no kind word!
Only a little flower came out,
And one small elegiac bird.

"THE BLOOM UPON THE GRAPE"

The bloom upon the grape I ask no more,
Nor pampered fragrance of the soft-lipped rose,
I only ask of Him who keeps the Door—
To open it for one who fearless goes
Into the dark, from which, reluctant, came
His innocent heart, a little laughing flame;
I only ask that he who gave me sight,
Who gave me hearing and who gave me breath,
Give me the last gift in His flaming hand—
The holy gift of Death.

THE FRIEND

Through the dark wood
There came to me a friend,
Bringing in his cold hands
Two words—'The End.'

His face was fair
As fading autumn flowers,
And the lost joy
Of unforgotten hours.

His voice was sweet
As rain upon a grave;
'Be brave,' he smiled.
And yet again—'be brave.'

ADORATION

Ah, if you worship anything,
In deepest hush of silence bend
The lone adoring knee,
And only silence bring
Into the sanctuary.
Trust not the fairest word
Your soul to wrong:
Even the Rose's bird
Hath not a song
Sweet as the silence
Round about the Rose.
Ah, something goes,
Fails, and is lost in speech
That silence knows.
How should I speak
The hush about my heart
That holds your name
Shrined in a burning core
Of central flame,
Like names of seraphim
Mystically writ on cloud?
To speak your name aloud
Were to unhallow
Such a holy thing;
Therefore I bring
To your white feet
And your immortal eyes
Silence forever,
But in such a wise
Am silent as the quiet waters are,
Hiding some holy star
Amid hushed lilies
In a secret lake.
Ah, if a ripple break
The stillness halcyon—
The star is gone!

"AT LAST I GOT A LETTER FROM THE DEAD"

At last I got a letter from the dead,
And out of it there fell a little flower,—
The violet of an unforgotten hour.

IV

SONGS FOR FRAGOLETTA

I

Fragoletta, blessed one,
What think you of the light of the sun?
Do you think the dark was best,
Lying snug in mother's breast?
Ah! I knew that sweetness, too,
Fragoletta, before you!
But, Fragoletta, now you're born,
You must learn to love the morn,
Love the lovely working light,
Love the miracle of sight,
Love the thousand things to do—
Little girl, I envy you!—
Love the thousand things to see,
Love your mother, and—love me!
And some night, Fragoletta, soon,
I'll take you out to see the moon;
And for the first time, child of ours,
You shall—think of it!—look on flowers,
And smell them, too, if you are good,
And hear the green leaves in the wood
Talking, talking, all together
In the happy windy weather;
And if the journey's not too far
For little limbs so lately made,
Limb upon limb like petals laid,
We'll go and picnic in a star.

II

Blue eyes looking up at me,
I wonder what you really see,
Lying in your cradle there,
Fragrant as a branch of myrrh.
Helpless little hands and feet,
O so helpless! O so sweet!
Tiny tongue that cannot talk,
Tiny feet that cannot walk,
Nothing of you that can do
Aught, except those eyes of blue.
How they open, how they close!

Eyelids of the baby-rose,
Open and shut, so blue, so wise,
Baby-eyelids, baby-eyes.

III

That, Fragoletta, is the rain
Beating upon the window-pane;
But lo! the golden sun appears,
To kiss away the window's tears.
That, Fragoletta, is the wind
That rattles so the window-blind;
And yonder shining thing's a star,
Blue eyes,—you seem ten times as far.
That, Fragoletta, is a bird
That speaks, yet never says a word;
Upon a cherry-tree it sings,
Simple as all mysterious things;
Its little life to peck and pipe
As long as cherries ripe and ripe,
And minister unto the need
Of baby-birds that feed and feed.
This, Fragoletta, is a flower,
Open and fragrant for an hour,
A flower, a transitory thing,
Each petal fleeting as a wing,
All a May morning blows and blows,
And then for everlasting goes.

IV

Blue eyes, against the whiteness pressed
Of little mother's hallowed breast,
The while your trembling lips are fed,
Look up at mother's bended head,
All benediction over you—
blue eyes looking into blue!
Fragoletta is so small,
We wonder that she lives at all—
Tiny alabaster girl,
Hardly bigger than a pearl;
That is why we take such care,
Lest someone runs away with her.

V

A BALLAD OF WOMAN

Gratefully Dedicated to Mrs. Pankhurst

She bore us in her dreaming womb,
And laughed into the face of Death;
She laughed, in her strange agony,—
To give her little baby breath.

Then, by some holy mystery,
She fed us from her sacred breast,
Soothed us with little birdlike words—
To rest—to rest—to rest—to rest;

Yea, softly fed us with her life—
Her bosom like the world in May:
Can it be true that men, thus fed,
Feed women—as I hear them say?

Long ere we grew to girl and boy,
She sewed the little things we wore,
And smiled unto herself for joy—
Mysterious Portress of the Door.

Shall she who bore the son of God,
And made the rose of Sappho's song,
She who saved France, and beat the drum
Of freedom, brook this vulgar wrong?

I wonder if such men as these
Had once a sister with blue eyes,
Kind as the soothing hand of God,
And as the quiet heaven wise.

I wonder if they ever saw
A soldier lying on a bed
On some lone battle-field, and watched
Some holy woman bind his head.

I wonder if they ever walked,
Lost in a black and weary land,
And suddenly a flower came
And took them softly by the hand.

I wonder if they ever heard
The silver scream, in some grey morn,

High in a lit and listening tower,
Because a man-child then was born.

I wonder if they ever saw
A woman's hair, or in her eye
Read the eternal mystery—
Or ever saw a woman die.

I wonder, when all friends had gone,—
The gay companions, the brave men—
If in some fragile girl they found
Their only stay and comrade then.

She who thus went through flaming hell
To make us, put into our clay
All that there is of heaven, shall she—
Mother and sister, wife and fay,—

Have no part in the world she made—
Serf of the rainbow, vassal flower—
Save knitting in the afternoon,
And rocking cradles, hour by hour!

AN EASTER HYMN

Spake the Lord Christ—"I will arise."
It seemed a saying void and vain—
How shall a dead man rise again!—
Vain as our tears, vain as our cries.
Not one of all the little band
That loved Him this might understand.

"I will arise"—Lord Jesus said.
Hearken, amid the morning dew,
Mary, a voice that calleth you,—
Then Mary turned her golden head,
And lo! all shining at her side
Her Master they had crucified.

At dawn to his dim sepulchre,
Mary, remembering that far day,
When at his feet the spikenard lay,
Came, bringing balm and spice and myrrh;
To her the grave had made reply:
"He is not here—He cannot die."

Praetor and priest in vain conspire,
Jerusalem and Rome in vain
Torture the god with mortal pain,
To quench that seed of living fire;
But light that had in heaven its birth
Can never be put out oh earth.

"I will arise"—across the years,
Even as to Mary that grey morn,
To us that gentle voice is borne—
"I will arise." He that hath ears
O hearken well this mystic word,
Let not the Master speak unheard.

No soul descended deep in hell,
The child of sorrow, sin and death,
The immortal spirit suffereth
To see corruption; though it fell
From loftiest station in the skies,
It still to heaven again must rise.

No dream of faith, no seed of love,
No lonely action nobly done,
But is as stable as the sun,
And fed and watered from above;
From nether base to starry cope
Nature's two laws are Faith and Hope.

Safe in the care of heavenly powers,
The good we dreamed but might not do,
Lost beauty magically new,
Shall spring as surely as the flowers,
When, 'mid the sobbing of the rain,
The heart of April beats again.

Celestial spirit that doth roll
The heart's sepulchral stone away,
Be this our resurrection day,
The singing Easter of the soul:
O Gentle Master of the Wise
Teach us to say, "I will arise."

BALLAD OF THE SEVEN O'CLOCK WHISTLE

The daisied dawn is in the sky,
And the young day still dew and dream,

When on the innocent morning air
There comes a terrifying scream;

And the four ends of the sad earth
Repeat the hellish dreadful call;
Soft ladies murmur in soft beds—
"The morning whistle—that is all!"

And I too turn to sleep once more,
A haunted sleep all filled with pain;
For in my sleep I see the men,
The victims of colossal Gain,

Troop in the doors of servitude;
I see the children weary-eyed,
I see the time-clock, and I see
The endless day that glooms inside.

It is the Moloch of the dawn,
Capital calling for its prey—
Men, women and little boys and girls,
It's human sacrifice each day.

And, as I hear that dreadful scream,
High in the dawn all filled with song,—
I pray within my aching heart—"O Lord!
O Lord! How long! How long!"

MORALITY

Give me the lifted skirt,
And the brave ways of wrong,
The fist, the dagger and the sword,
And the out-spoken song.

Ah! bring me not the love
That bargains, bids and buys:
For so much loving I will give
So much in lips and eyes;

But love with bosom bared,
Sweet as a bird and wild,
That in her savage maidenhood
Cries for a little child.

VI

FOR THE BIRTHDAY OF EDGAR ALLAN POE

January 19, 1909

Poet of doom, dementia, and death,
Of beauty singing in a charnel house,
Like the lost soul of a poor moon-mad maid,
With too much loving of some lord of hell;
Doomed and disastrous spirit, to what shore
Of what dark gulf infernal art thou strayed,
Or to what spectral star of topless heaven
Art lifted and enthroned?

The winter dark,
And the drear winter cold that welcomed thee
To a world all winter, gird with ice and storm
Thy January day—yea! the same world
Of winter and the wintry hearts of men;
And still, for all thy shining, the same swarm
That mocked thy song gather about thy fame,
With the small murmur of the undying worm,
And whisper, blind and foul, amid thy dust.

TO RALPH WALDO EMERSON

Poet, whose words are like the tight-packed seed
Sealed in the capsule of a silver flower,
Still at your art we wonder as we read,
The art dynamic charging each word with power.

Seeds of the silver flower of Emerson:
One, on the winds to Scotland brought, did sink
In Carlyle's heart; and one was lately blown
To Belgium, and flowered in—Maeterlinck.

RICHARD WATSON GILDER

Obiit Nov. 18, 1909

America grows poorer day by day—
Richer and richer, I have heard some say:

They thought of a poor wealth I do not heed—
For, one by one, the men who dreamed the dream
That was America, and is now no more,
Have gone in flame through that mysterious door,
And scarcely one remains, in all our need.

The dream goes with the dreamer—ah! beware,
Country of facile silver and of gold,
To slight the gentle strength of a pure prayer;
America, all made out of a dream—
A dream of good men in the days of old;
What if the dream should fade and none remain
To tell your children the old dream again!

Therefore, with laurel and with tears and rue,
Stand by his grave this sad November day,
Sadder that he untimely goes away,
Who sang and wrought so well for that high dream
We call America—the world made new,
New with clean hope and faith and purpose true.

Gilder, your name, with each return of Spring,
Shall write itself in the soft April flowers,
And, when you hear the murmur of bright showers
Over your sleep, and little lives that sing
Come back once more, know that the rainbowed rain
Is but our tears, saying: "Come back again."

IN A COPY OF FITZGERALD'S "OMAR"

A little book, this grim November day,
Wherein, O tired heart, to creep away,—
Come drink this wine and wear this fadeless rose,
Nor heed the world, nor what the world shall say.

A thousand gardens—yet to-day there blows
In all their wintry walks no single rose,
But here with Omar you shall find the Spring
That fears no Autumn and eternal glows.

So on the song-soft petals of his rhyme
Pillow your head, as in some golden clime,
And let the beauty of eternity
Smooth from your brow the little frets of time.

VII

A BALLAD OF TOO MUCH BEAUTY

There is too much beauty upon this earth
For lonely men to bear,
Too many eyes, too enchanted skies,
Too many things too fair;
And the man who would live the life of a man
Must turn his eyes away—if he can.

He must not look at the dawning day,
Or watch the rising moon;
From the little feet, so white, so fleet,
He must turn his eyes away;
And the flowers and the faces he must pass by
With stern self-sacrificing eye.

For beauty and duty are strangers forever,
Work and wonder ever apart,
And the laws of life eternally sever
The ways of the brain from the ways of the heart;
Be it flower or pearl, or the face of a girl,
Or the ways of the waters as they swirl.

Lo! beauty is sorrow, and sorrowful men
Have no heart to look on the face of the sky,
Or hear the remorseful voice of the sea,
Or the song of the wandering wind in the tree,
Or even watch a butterfly.

SPRING IN THE PARIS CATACOMBS

I saw strange bones to-day in Paris town,
Deep in the quarried dark, while over-head
The roar of glad and busy things went by—
Over our heads—
So many heads—
Deep down, deep down—
Those strange old bones deep down in Paris town:
Heads where no longer dwell—
Yet who shall tell!—
Such thoughts as those
That make a rose
Of a maid's cheek,

Filling it with such bloom—
All fearless of the unsuspected doom—
As flood wild April with such hushing breath
That Death himself believes no more in Death.

Yea! I went down
Out of the chestnuts and the girl-filled town,
Only a yard or two beneath the street,
Haunted a little while by little feet,
Going, did they but know, the self-same way
As all those bones as white as the white May
That roofs the orchards overhead with bloom.

Perhaps I only dreamed,
And yet to me it seemed
That those old bones talked strangely each to each,
Chattering together in forgotten speech—

Speaking of Her
That was so very fair,
Telling of Him
So strong
He is a song
Up there in the far day, where even yet
Fools sing of fates and faces
Even fools cannot forget.

Faces went by, as haughty as of old,
Wearing upon their heads the unminted gold
That flowers in blackness only,
And sad lips smiled softly, softly,
Knowing well it was too late
Even for Fate.

Yet one shape that I never can forget
Waved a wild sceptre at me, ruling yet
An empire gone where all empires must go,
Melting away as simply as the snow;
Yet no one heeded the flower of his menace,
As little heeded him as that One Face
That suddenly I saw go wandering by,
And saying as she went—"I—still—am—I!"

And the dry bones thereat
Rattled together, laughing, gossipping
Together in the gloom
That dared not sing,

The little trivial gossip of the tomb—
Ah! just as long ago, in their dry way,
They mocked at fairy faces and strong eyes
That of their foolish loving make us wise.

Paris: May, 1913.

A FACE IN A BOOK

In an old book I found her face
Writ by a dead man long ago—
I found, and then I lost the place;
So nothing but her face I know,
And her soft name writ fair below.

Even if she lived I cannot learn,
Or but a dead man's dream she were;
Page after yellow page I turn,
But cannot come again to her,
Although I know she must be there.

On other books of other men,
Far in the night, year-long, I pore,
Hoping to find her face again,
Too fair a face to see no more—
And 'twas so soft a name she bore.

Sometimes I think the book was Youth,
And the dead man that wrote it I,
The face was Beauty, the name Truth—
And thus, with an unseeing eye,
I pass the long-sought image by.

TIME, BEAUTY'S FRIEND

"Is she still beautiful?" I asked of one
Who of the unforgotten faces told
That for long years I had not looked upon—
"Beautiful still—but she is growing old";
And for a space I sorrowed, thinking on
That face of April gold.

Then up the summer night the moon arose,
Glassing her sacred beauty in the sea,

That ever at her feet in silver flows;
And with her rising came a thought to me—
How ever old and ever young she grows,
And still more lovely she.

Thereat I smiled, thinking on lovely things
That dateless and immortal beauty wear,
Whereof the song immortal tireless sings,
And Time but touches to make lovelier;
On Beauty sempiternal as the Spring's—
So old are all things fair.

Then for that face I cast aside my fears,
For changing Time is Beauty's changeless friend,
That never reaches but for ever nears,
Tireless the old perfections to transcend,
Fairness more fair to fashion with the years,
And loveliest to end.

YOUNG LOVE

Young love, all rainbows in the lane,
Brushed by the honeysuckle vines,
Scattered the wild rose in a dream:
A sweeter thing his arm entwines.

Ah, redder lips than any rose!
Ah, sweeter breath than any bee
Sucks from the heart of any flower;
Ah, bosom like the Summer sea!

A fairy creature made of dew
And moonrise and the songs of birds,
And laughter like the running brook,
And little soft, heart-broken words.

Haunted as marble in the moon,
Her whiteness lies on young love's breast.
And living frankincense and myrrh
Her lips that on his lips are pressed.

Her eyes are lost within his eyes,
His eyes in hers are fathoms deep;
Death is not stiller than these twain
That smile as in a magic sleep.

I heard him say as they went by,
Two human flowers in the dew:
"Darling, ah, God, if you should die,
You know, that moment I die, too."

I heard her say: "I could not live
An hour without you"; heard her say:
"My life is in your hands to keep,
To keep, or just to throw away."

I heard him say: "For just us two
The world was made, the stars above
Move in their orbits, to this end:
That you and I should meet and love."

I heard her say: "And God himself
Has us in keeping, heart to heart;
In his great book our names are writ—
The Book of Those that Never Part."

"How strange it is!" I heard him say;
"How strange!" and yet again, "How strange!
To meet at last, and know this love
Of ours can never fade or change."

"How strange to think that you are mine,
Each little hair of your dear head,
And no one else's in the world—
How strange it is!" the woman said.

I stand aside to let them pass,
My Autumn face they never see;
Their eyes are on the rising sun,
But 'tis the setting sun for me.

For me no wild rose in the lane,
But only sad autumnal flowers,
And falling shadows and old sighs,
And melancholy drift of hours!

LOVERS

They sit within a woodland place,
Trellised with rustling light and shade;
So like a spirit is her face
That he is half afraid

To speak—lest she should fade.

Mysterious, beneath the boughs,
Like two enchanted shapes, they are,
Whom Love hath builded them a house
Of little leaf and star,
And the brown evening jar.

So lovely and so strange a thing
Each is to each to look upon,
They dare not hearken a bird sing,
Or from the other one
Take eyes—lest they be gone.

So still—the watching woodland peers
And pecks about them, butterflies
Light on her hand—a flower; eve hears
Two questions, two replies—
O love that never dies!

FOR A PICTURE BY ROSE CECIL O'NEIL

Kisses are long forgotten of this twain,
Kisses and words—the sweet small prophecies
That run before the Lord of Love: the fain
Touch of the hand, and feasting of the eyes,
All tendrilled sweets that blossom at the door
Of the stern doom, whose ecstacy is this—
The end of all small speech of word or kiss,
And whose strange name is Love—and one name more.

One is this twain past power of speech to tell,
Each lost in each, and each for ever found;
Drained is the cup that holds both heaven and hell;
Peace deep as peace of those divinely drowned
In leagues of moonlit water wraps them round,
And it is well with them—yea! it is well.

LOVE IN SPAIN

You shall not dare to drink this cup,
Yet fear this other I hold up—
Sings Love in Spain:

One brimming deep with woman's breath—
This other moon-lit cup is Death;
Drink one, drink twain.

No sippers we of ladies' lips,
Toyers of amorous finger tips,
Are we in Spain.

Terrible like a bright sweet sword,
And little tender is the Lord
Of Love in Spain.

His song a tiger-throated thing,—
A crouch, a cry, a frightened string;
Death the refrain.

Scarlet and lightning are its words,
There is no room in it for birds
And flowers in Spain.

A flash, and mouth is lost on mouth,
And life on life; so in the South
The cup we drain.

We do not dream and hesitate
About its brim; we fear not Fate
That love in Spain.

And ah! come hear the reason why—
There are no girls beneath the sky
Like those of Spain.

All other women scarcely seem
More than pale women in a dream
By ours of Spain.

Ah! who aright shall tell their praise,—
Their subtle, soft, imperious ways,
Their high disdain.

Golden as bars of Spanish gold,
Hot as the sun, as the moon cold,
The girls of Spain.

Their faces as magnolias white,
Their hair the soul of summer night,
Soft as soft rain;

And swift as the steel blade that flies
Into a coward's heart their eyes,
Then soft again.

Under their little languid feet,
That carry such a world of sweet,
My heart lies slain.

Girls North and South, and East and West,
But fairer far than all the rest
The girls of Spain.

THE EYES THAT COME FROM IRELAND

Don't you love the eyes that come from Ireland?
The grey-blue eyes so strangely grey and blue,
The fighting loving eyes,
The eyes that tell no lies—
Don't you love the eyes that come from Ireland?

Don't you love the eyes that come from Ireland?
The dreaming mocking eyes that see you through,
The eyes that smile and smile,
With the heart-break all the while,—
Don't you love the eyes that come from Ireland?

Don't you love the eyes that come from Ireland?
The eyes that hate of England made so blue,
The mystic eyes that see
More than Saxon you and me—
Don't you love the eyes that come from Ireland?

A BALLAD OF THE KIND LITTLE CREATURES

I had no where to go,
I had no money to spend:
"O come with me," the Beaver said,
"I live at the world's end."

"Does the world ever end!"
To the Beaver then said I:
"O yes! the green world ends," he said,
"Up there in the blue sky."

I walked along with him to home,
At the edge of a singing stream—
The little faces in the town
Seemed made out of a dream.

I sat down in the little house,
And ate with the kind things—
Then suddenly a bird comes out
Of the bushes, and he sings:

"Have you no home? O take my nest,
It almost is the sky;"
And then there came along the creek
A purple dragon-fly.

"Have you no home?" he said;
"O come along with me,
Get on my wings—the moon's my home"—
The dragon-fly said he.

The Bee was told by a young Bat
A man had need of home;
He flew away at once, and said
"Come to my honeycomb!"

Even the butterfly,
A painted hour;
Said to the homeless one:
"I know a flower."

The Ant came slowly,
Late, of course, but still
Bringing the tiny welcome
Of his hill.

The tired turtle,
Fumbling through the wood,
Came, asking hospitably
"If I would?"

Even a hornet came,
With sheathed sting,—
He never yet had seen
So lost a thing!

There was his nest
Up in the singing boughs,
Among the pears,

A fragrant humming house.

And even little
Stupid things that crawl
Among the reeds, deeming
That that is all,
Came a long weary way
To bid me home.

A snake said:
"In the world there is a place
Where you can lie
And dream of her white face."

The moss said: "Your blue eyes
Need my green sleep";
The willow said: "Ah! when
You weep I weep."

Wonderful earth
Of little kindly things,
That buzz and beam
And flitter little wings!

Over the sexton's grave
The growing grass
Cried out: "Come home!
I am alive, alas!"

ENVOI

Ah! love, the world is fading,
Flower by flower,
Each has his little house,
And each his hour.

The ship rocked long
Across the weary sea,
But at the last
There is a port for me.

BLUE FLOWER

Blue flower waving in the wind,
Say whose blue eyes

Lift up your swaying fragile stem
To the blue skies.

Is she a queen that lies asleep
In a green hill,
With all her silver ornaments
Around her still?

Or is she but a simple girl,
Whose boy was drowned,
In some cold sea, some stormy morn,
On some blue sound?

THE HEART UNSEEN

So many times the heart can break,
So many ways,
Yet beat along and beat along
So many days.

A fluttering thing we never see,
And only hear
When some stern doctor to our side
Presses his ear.

Strange hidden thing, that beats and beats
We know not why,
And makes us live, though we indeed
Would rather die.

Mysterious, fighting, loving thing,
So sad, so true—
I would my laughing eyes some day
Might look on you.

THE SHIMMER OF THE SOUND

In the long shimmer of the Sound
May I some day be laughing found,
Part of its restless to and fro,
A humble worker of the tides
That round the sleepless planet flow,
And in the rock and drift of things—

O how the sea-weed sways and swings!
Is it her hair—has she been found
In the long shimmer of the Sound!

Do some small task I do not know—
O maybe help the mussel grow,
Or tint the shell-imprisoned pearl—

A mute companion of the waves
That toss within their moonlit graves—
Is it a king, or but a girl?

And, all the while, she sings and sings,
And waves her wild white hands with glee,
Mysterious sister of the world,
That singing water called the sea.

O tell me was this sea-weed found
In the long shimmer of the Sound!

A SONG OF SINGERS

Singers all along the street,
Singing every kind of song—
One man's song is honey-sweet,
One man's song is hammer-strong;
Yet, however sweet the singing,
However strong the hammer-swinging,—
All the bees are round that honey
Which the vulgar world calls money.

Singers all along the street—
One sings Love and one sings Death,
Roses sings one and little feet,
And one sings wine with fevered breath;
Yet all the bees are round that honey
Which the vulgar world calls money.

Singers singing down the street,
I believe there is a song,
Could you sing it, that would beat
All the sweet and all the strong;
Just a simple song of pity,
'Mid the iron of the city.

Singers all the street along,

There is still another song
All the world is waiting, breathless,
Just to hear some poet singing,
Song of something gay and deathless
'Mid the grinding dark endeavour
That goes on and on for ever,
Something more than mere words bringing,

Something more than butterflies,
Or the sugared ancient lies,
Something with the ring of truth,
And the majesty of youth,
Something singing "all is well"
In the blackest pit of hell!

O we are so tired of birds,
Of rainbows and the love-sick words!
Sing us but some manly tune,
Leaving out the rising moon
Sing the song of Hope Eternal
In the face of Facts Infernal,
And make your singing somehow prove it—
Faith so firm no doubt can move it—
Then the bees will leave the honey
Which the vulgar world calls money.

THE END

Tell me, strange heart, so mysteriously beating—
Unto what end?
Body and soul so mysteriously meeting,
Strange friend and friend;
Hand clasped in hand so mysteriously faring,
Say what and why all this dreaming and daring,
This sowing and reaping and laughing and weeping,
That ends but in sleeping—
Only one meaning, only—the End.

Ah! all the love, the gold glory, the singing,—
Unto what end?
Flowers of April immortally springing,
Face of one's friend,
Stars of the morning and moon in her quarters,
Shining of suns and running of waters,
Growing and blowing and snowing and flowing,—
Ah! where are they going?
All on one journey, all to—the End.

My Ladies' Sonnets and Other Vain and Amatorious Verses (1887)
Volumes in Folio (1889) poems
George Meredith: Some Characteristics (1890)
The Book-Bills of Narcissus (1891)
English Poems (1892)
The Religion of a Literary Man (1893)
Robert Louis Stevenson: An Elegy and Other Poems (1895)
Quest of the Golden Girl (1896) novel
Prose Fancies (1896)
Retrospective Reviews (1896)
Rubaiyat of Omar Khayyam (1897)
If I Were God (1897)
The Romance of Zion Chapel (1898)
In Praise of Bishop Valentine (1898)
Young Lives (1899)
Sleeping Beauty and Other Prose Fancies (1900)
The Worshipper of The Image (1900)
The Love Letters of the King, or The Life Romantic (1901)
An Old Country House (1902)
Odes from the Divan of Hafiz (1903) translation
Old Love Stories Retold (1904)
Painted Shadows (1904)
Romances of Old France (1905)
Little Dinners with the Sphinx and other Prose Fancies (1907)
Omar Repentant (1908)
Wagner's Tristan and Isolde (1909) Translator
Attitudes and Avowals (1910) essays
October Vagabonds (1910)
New Poems (1910)
The Maker of Rainbows and Other Fairy-Tales and Fables (1912)
The Lonely Dancer and Other Poems (1913)
The Highway to Happiness (1913)
Vanishing Roads and Other Essays (1915)
The Silk-Hat Soldier and Other Poems in War Time (1915)
The Chain Invisible (1916)
Pieces of Eight (1918)
The Junk-Man and Other Poems (1920)
A Jongleur Strayed (1922) poems
Woodstock: An Essay (1923)
The Romantic '90s (1925) memoirs
The Romance of Perfume (1928)
There Was a Ship (1930)
From a Paris Garret (1936) memoirs

The Diary of Samuel Pepys (editor)